THE JOKE'S ON ME...!

To Bill
My Good Friend,

Also by Mel Simons:

The Old-Time Radio Trivia Book
The Old-Time Television Trivia Book
Old-Time Radio Memories
The Show-Biz Trivia Book
Old-Time Television Memories
The Movie Trivia Book
Voices from the Philco
The Good Music Trivia Book
The Mel Simons Joke Book: If It's Laughter You're After
The Old-Time Radio Trivia Book II
The Comedians Trivia Book
The Old-Time Radio Trivia Book III
Take These Jokes Please
The Old-Time Radio Trivia Book IV
The Old-Time Television Trivia Book II
The Old-Time Radio Trivia Book V
The Old-Time Television Trivia Book III

THE JOKE'S ON ME...!

BY MEL SIMONS

BearManor Media
2018

The Joke's On Me…!

© 2018 Mel Simons

All rights reserved.

For information, address:

BearManor Media
P. O. Box 71426
Albany, GA 31708

bearmanormedia.com

Typesetting and layout by John Teehan

Published in the USA by BearManor Media

ISBN — 978-1-62933-295-6

Dedication

This book is dedicated to my good friend Jan Hernstat. We share a love for the great 20th century singer Al Jolson.

Jan is the president of the International Al Jolson Society.

Mel Simons

www.melsimons.net

The Joke's On Me...!

Marty Allen

Foreword

"Hello Dere"

Mel Simons is a brilliant comedic writer. His knowledge is a rare tribute to the comedy stars of today and yesteryears.

If you read all of his many books, you'll know and live and laugh at the real show business, and admire the men and women that brought them to you

Sincere good wishes,

Marty Allen
Allen and Rossi

The Joke's On Me...!

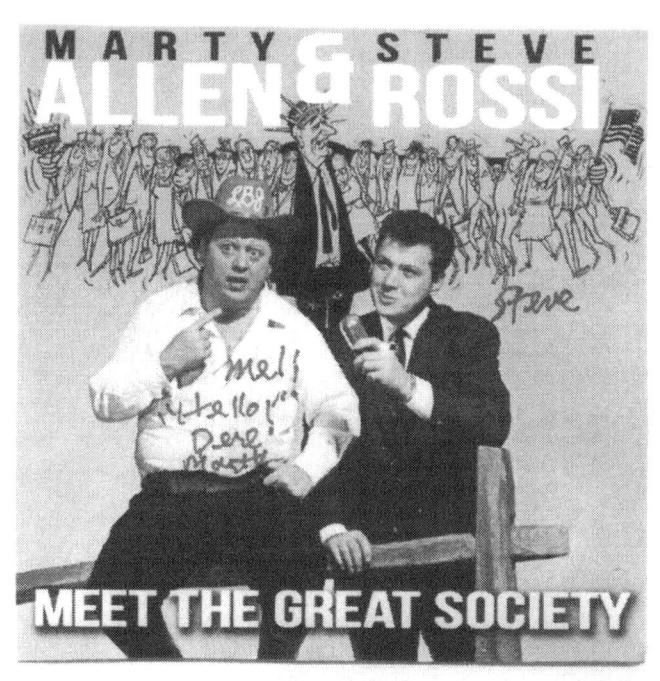

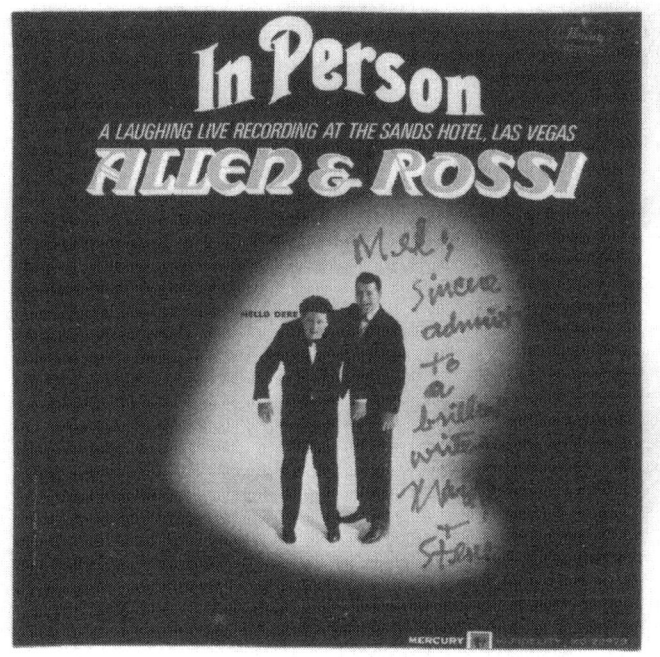

The Joke's On Me...!

Jokes

There is a stuttering jeweler who runs a little shop. A customer rushes in and says, "Take this watch and have it cleaned. Put in a new movement and put in a news trap. I'll be back in thirty minutes." As the man is about to rush out, the jeweler looks up and says, "C-c-c-c come in."

A fellow, to stay in business, always insisted on having his checks dated ahead. So the bank let him do it. But, even with that advantage, he died. His tombstone read: "Here lies the body of Harold Sherman, died April 23 as of May 2."

A Lufthansa jet goes down and lands in the ocean five miles from Germany. The captain announces over the microphone, "Ladies and gentlemen. All those who can swim, use the emergency exit and start swimming. You are only five miles from shore. All those who can't swim… thank you for flying Lufthansa!"

The Joke's On Me...!

Red Buttons

Red Buttons Jokes

Dolly Parton, who said to Mrs. Olson, "Yes, they're mountain grown"... never got a dinner.

King Solomon, who said to his thousand wives, "Who doesn't have a headache tonight?"... never got a dinner.

Ben Hur, who said to his sister Ben Him, "You wanna switch?" and Ben Him, who said to Ben Hur, "If I do, I'll be Ben Gay"... never got a dinner.

Uncle Remus, who once said to Uncle Ben, "You're a credit to your rice"... never got a dinner.

Lot, who said to his wife when she was turned into a pillar of salt, "Salt I got. Popcorn I need."... never got a dinner.

Sophia Loren's new baby, who said to Sophia, "Is that all for me?"... never got a dinner.

Adam, who said to Eve, "You better back up. I have no idea how big this thing gets"... never got a dinner.

Jimmy Carter, who said to Pope John, "Next time bring the missus"... never got a dinner.

The Joke's On Me...!

Vincent Van Gogh, who said to the hat salesman, "I like it, but it keeps sliding over my ear"... never got a dinner.

Alex the Great, who said on his wedding night, "It's only a nickname"... never got a dinner.

The Hunchback of Notre Dame, who said, "This isn't a hump. I ate a cantaloupe and it backed up on me"... never got a dinner.

John Wilkes Booth, who said, "I'm sorry. I thought he was a critic"... never got a dinner.

The Invisible Man, who said to his wife, "I don't care if it looks silly, don't stop"... never got a dinner.

Judge and Jury Jokes

Judge: "Has the jury reached a verdict?"
Foreman: "Yes, your honor. We, the jury, find the murderer not guilty."

The town drunk stood in front of the judge. The judge said, "My good man, you've been brought here for drinking." The drunk said, "Okay, Judge. Let's get started."

Judge: "I thought I told you I never wanted to see you again."
Criminal: "That's what I told the police, but they wouldn't listen."

The judge had just awarded a divorce to a wife who had charged nonsupport. The judge said to the husband, "I have decided to give your wife 200 dollars a month toward her support." The husband said, "Thanks, Judge. I'll try to throw in a few dollars myself."

Judge: "How long did it take your wife to learn to drive?"
Husband: "It will be ten years in September, Your Honor."

The Joke's On Me...!

Mel Simons and Jack Carter

6

Jack Carter Jokes

Phyllis Diller is beautiful. She is the only woman I know who gets obscene phone calls collect.

I once dated an older woman. I told her to act her age, so she died.

This lady had a big nose. She rolled over in bed. Her nose got caught in her ear. She sneezed and blew her brains out.

(To a heckler) I couldn't warm up to you if we were cremated together.

George Burns is so old he ordered a three-minute egg and the waitress wanted the money in advance.

George Jessel is an unhappy man. He just got his first anti-Semitic letter, and it was in Yiddish.

Jerry Lewis is a charitable man. Last year at an old-age home he gave them a tremendous donation – his mother and father.

Cute Quotes

Anyone who goes to a psychiatrist ought to have his head examined.
— Sam Goldwyn

I married a German. Every night I dress up as Poland and he invades me.
— Bette Midler

I can hold a note as long as the Chase National Bank.
— Ethel Merman

Beauty fades. Dumb is forever.
— Judge Judy

If I had as many love affairs as you fellows have given me credit for, I would now be speaking to you from inside a jar at the Harvard Medical School.
— Frank Sinatra

My husband was so ugly he used to stand outside the doctor's office and make people sick.
— Moms Mabley

By the time a man is wise enough to watch his step, he's too old to go anywhere.
— Billy Crystal

The Joke's On Me...!

I wanted to be the first woman to burn her bra, but it would have taken the fire department four days to put the fire out.
– Dolly Parton

Doing nothing is very hard to do. You never know when you're finished.
– Leslie Nielsen

It took me 17 years to get 3,000 hits in baseball. I did it in one afternoon on the golf course.
– Hank Aaron

Life is hard. It is much harder when you are stupid.
– John Wayne

I had some horse. The jockey kept a diary of the trip.
– Fred Astaire

My father originated the limbo dance, trying to get into a pay toilet.
– Slappy White

I'm not upset about my divorce. I'm only upset I'm not a widow.
– Roseanne Barr

The Joke's On Me...!

Soupy Sales

The Joke's On Me...!

Soupy Sale Jokes

I used to look like Cary Grant, but not after being hit with 19,000 pies.

Show me a toilet in a castle, and I'll show you a royal flush.

Do you know who the happiest man is after Christmas? Santa Claus, because he has the names of all the bad little girls.

Never hit a man when he's down. Kick him. It's easier.

One way to tell when you're having an earthquake is your Jell-o stands still.

Buy thermometers in the wintertime. They're much lower then.

Do unto others and then cut out.

There are usually two kinds of partygoers: One wants to leave early and one wants to stay late. The only trouble is they're usually married to each other.

People who eat sweets take up two seats.

The Joke's On Me...!

My Brother-In-Law

I have a brother-in-law named Bernie. He is a super friend. However, many strange things have happened to him from childhood on:

When Bernie was born, his father spent three weeks trying to find a loophole in his birth certificate.

His mother got morning sickness after he was born.

As a child, Bernie was a bed wetter. On his birthday his parents gave him an electric blanket.

One hot summer Bernie asked his mother to turn off the electric fan. She said, "Grab the blade."

His mother didn't like him. Once she took him to an orphanage and told him to mingle.

His parents always used to say to him, "Never take candy from a stranger, unless he offers you a ride."

When Bernie was nine, his family moved to Chicago, Illinois. When he was twelve, he found them.

He was never very good at sports. When he played in Little League, his father traded him to another team . . . for twenty dollars and a child to be born later.

He loved to play stickball. He played second sewer.

The Joke's On Me...!

When he played football, he was known as "Crazy Legs" until he was thirteen years old. That's when he learned to put his pants on with the zipper in front.

Bernie is now a married man. He takes vitamin E, and his wife takes iron pills. So when he's ready, she's rusty.

Bernie tried being a stock broker. He put me into two stocks. One was a revolving-door stock, the other was a toilet-tissue stock. He got wiped out before he could turn around.

He is now building a halfway house for girls who don't want to go all the way.

I'll never forget the time I went to visit Bernie. He had a bandage on each ear. I asked, "What happened to your ear?" He said, "I was doing some ironing, and the phone rang. I picked up the iron by mistake." I said, "Well, what happened to your other ear?" He said, "I had to call him back."

Bernie has now become a sex symbol for women who no longer care.

A couple of weeks ago, Bernie was complaining that he couldn't sell his car. I asked, "Well, why don't you turn back the speedometer?" I saw him yesterday and said to him, "Did you sell your car?" He said, "Are you crazy? I only have 5,000 miles on it."

One afternoon Bernie and I went to Fenway Park to see the Red Sox play the Yankees. Forty thousand people stood up to sing the National Anthem. An usher came down the aisle and told Bernie to stop singing. He was throwing the crowd off-key.

The Joke's On Me...!

Mel Simons and George Kirby

The Joke's On Me...!

Knock-Knock Jokes

Knock! Knock!
Who's there?
Honey bee.
Honey bee who?
Honey bee a dear and get me the remote.

Knock! Knock!
Who's there?
Hanna.
Hanna who?
Hanna partridge in a pear tree.

Knock! Knock!
Who's there?
Hatch.
Hatch who?
Are you catching a cold?

Knock! Knock!
Who's there?
Pecan.
Pecan who?
Pecan someone your own size.

The Joke's On Me...!

Knock! Knock!
Who's there?
Fish.
Fish who?
Fish you a Merry Christmas.

Knock! Knock!
Who's there?
Franz.
Franz who?
Franz, Romans, and Countrymen...!

Knock! Knock!
Who's there?
Lena.
Lena who?
Lena little closer. I want to tell you a secret.

Knock! Knock!
Who's there?
Police.
Police who?
Police stop telling these awful knock-knock jokes.

Doctor Jokes

A man goes to see his doctor. The man says, "Doc, I'm having a tough time controlling my bladder." The doctor says, "Get off of my new carpet."

A bent-over old lady hobbled into a doctor's office. She came out five minutes later standing perfectly straight. A man sitting in the waiting room said in amazement, "My God, I've never seen anything like it. What did the doctor do to you?" She said, "He gave me a longer cane."

A doctor gave a man six months to live. The man couldn't afford to pay his bill, so the doctor gave him another six months.

A lady goes to see a doctor. The doctor says, "Get undressed." She gets undressed. He says, "Lady, that's the ugliest body I've ever seen." She says, "That's what my doctor told me." He says, "What are you coming to me for?" She says, "I wanted another doctor's opinion."

My friend Harold went to see a proctologist. Being very curious, Harold asked him, "What made you become a proctologist?" The doctor answered, "I can't remember faces."

A doctor asked his patient, "Is there anything you'd like to ask me?" The patient replied, "Well, I was thinking about getting a vasectomy. What do you think?" The doctor said, "That's a big decision. Have you talked it over with your family?" The patient answered, "Yes, we took a vote. They're in favor of it 17 to 2."

The Joke's On Me...!

Robin Williams

Robin Williams Jokes

We had gay burglars the other night. They broke in and rearranged the furniture.

I went to rehab for alcoholism in wine country, just to keep my options open.

Why do they call it rush hour when nothing moves?

Did you ever look at Don King and think that he might be Buckwheat's illegitimate child?

Death is nature's way of saying, "Your table's ready."

If women ran the world, we wouldn't have wars, just intense negotiations every 28 days.

If it's the Psychic Network, why do they need a phone number?

Cocaine is God's way of saying that you're making too much money.

The Joke's On Me...!

Mel Simons and Jan Murray

Jan Murray Jokes

You know it's going to be a bad day if you wake up with your waterbed busted, and you know you ain't got a waterbed.

Invitations were extended to this dinner for Frank Sinatra in an unusual fashion. A guy drove up in a cement truck and asked for my shoe size.

Sinatra invited me to live here at the Waldorf with him. "Live my life," he said. My heart said "Yes," but my prostate said "No."

Milton Berle was abandoned by wolves and reared by his parents. His parents hated him. When he was four years old, his mother and father were still trying to get an abortion. But he's a good guy. He's really a humanitarian. He'll help anybody, but so does the Heimlich maneuver.

I once suffered from senility, but I forgot about it.

I know this guy who's a gift to humanity, and so is Kaopectate.

The Joke's On Me...!

Myron Cohen and Mel Simons

Myron Cohen Jokes

A couple has been married for thirty years, and for thirty years it's been murder. Finally, they come to the bar of justice. The judge listens to them and says, "Come into my chambers. I recommend reconciliation in this case." The wife looked at the judge with daggers in her eyes and said, "I wouldn't give him a reconciliation if he should drop dead. Why, for thirty years he ate my heart out, gave me ulcers. Why only in the last six months I lost twenty-five pounds with him, that bum." Whereupon the judge said, "Do you want an immediate decree?" She said, "Your Honor, let me lose another five pounds first."

This fellow comes home and finds his wife in a compromising position with a stranger. He says, "What the hell is going on here?" His wife turns to the stranger and asks, "Didn't I tell you he was stupid?"

A drunk is driving his car the wrong way on a one-way street. A cop stops him and says, "Where the devil do you think you are? Didn't you see the arrows?" He replied, "I didn't even see the Indians."

A man wrote a letter to the Internal Revenue Service. It said, "On my recent tax return, I cheated. I've had a guilty conscience ever since and haven't been able to sleep. Enclosed you will find a check in the amount of five thousand dollars. If I still can't sleep, I'll send you the balance."

The Joke's On Me...!

This adorable little great-grandma was walking down the street. She's in her late eighties. A young doctor came along and said, "Hello, Mrs. Levine. How do you feel?" She said, "I'll tell you the truth, hurts me the pressure, and the arthritis and my ears, and my stomach hurts." The doctor said, "Why don't you come to the office to see me?" She responded, "Maybe next week when I feel better."

This man worked in a dress factory. For twenty years he would walk in for work at eight o'clock. Every morning at eight o'clock for twenty years. This one morning he walked in at nine o'clock. He was cut to ribbons, two black eyes, bloody nose, clothes torn to shreds. The boss asked, "What happened to you?" He responded, "I fell down a whole flight of stairs. I almost got killed." The boss said, "So this took an hour?"

The Joke's On Me…!

Jonathan Winters

The Joke's On Me...!

Totie Fields

Totie Fields Jokes

I've been on a diet for two weeks, and all I've lost is fourteen days.

A diet is a system of starving yourself to death so you can live a little longer.

Where do people go for aggravation who have no children?

Would you like to wake up every day with a smile on your face? Go to sleep every night with a coat hanger in your mouth.

Shirley Temple had charisma as a child, but it cleared up an as adult.

Do you like to shop? Do you like bargains? I do. The other day I bought twenty pairs of pantyhose for fifteen cents apiece. They had the seam running up the front. What can you do? I figured I'd learn to walk backwards.

I went into a department store and tried on a girdle that was decorated with tiny rosebuds. When I got it on, the roses opened up in full bloom.

The Joke's On Me...!

Jack Carter – Pat Henry – Myron Cohen

Pat Henry – Myron Cohen – Henny Youngman

The Joke's On Me...!

Bar Jokes

My friend Irving walked into a bar and ordered a double. The bartender brought out a guy who looked just like Irving.

A guy walks into a bar and there's a guy dead drunk there. He figures he'll be a good Samaritan and take him home. So he takes him off the bar stool, and the guy falls down. He picks the drunk up and starts to walk him out of the place. Three times the drunk falls down on the way to the door. He finally gets him into his car. He gets to the front of the guy's house, drags him out of the car, walks him to his door, and the guy falls down about four times. Finally he rings the doorbell, and the guy's wife comes to the door. He says, "I brought your husband home." She asked, "Where's his wheelchair?"

A German walks into a bar and asks for a martini. The bartender asks, "Dry?" The German replies, "Nein, just one."

A drunk walks into a bar and yells at the bartender, "I slept with your mother." The bartender yells back, "Dad, you're drunk again. Go home."

Take These Jokes, Please!

Louis Nye

Lawyer Jokes

A convict was sentenced to die in the electric chair. He called his lawyer for some advice. The lawyer replied, "Don't sit down."

How do you save a drowning lawyer? Take your foot off his head.

A ninety-five-year-old couple went to a lawyer for a divorce. When they were asked why they waited so long, the old man said, "We wanted to wait until all the kids had died."

What does a lawyer use for birth control? His personality.

If you can't find a lawyer who knows the law, find a lawyer who knows the judge.

A man walked into a lawyer's office and said, "What are your rates?" The lawyer said "$200 for three questions." The man asked, "Isn't that rather steep?" "Yes," said the lawyer. "And what is your third question?"

What do you need when you have three lawyers up to their necks in cement? More cement!

Take These Jokes, Please!

Jerry Lewis

Jerry Lewis Jokes

When an Arab oil sheik was leaving for a trip to the United States, his wife told him to bring her back a little something cute in silk. So he brought her three jockeys from Aquaduct.

Do you know what a wrench is? It's where Jewish cowboys live.

A man is sitting in a car that's crashed into a tree. He's cut and bleeding. A cop asks, "Are you comfortable?" The man responds, "I make a nice living."

The doctor told me I had a dual personality. Then he laid an eighty-two dollar bill on me. So I gave him his forty-one bucks, and said, "Get the other forty-one bucks from the other guy."

The last time I went to New York it was incredible. We circled the airport for hours. What made it incredible is we were on a bus.

Take These Jokes, Please!

Paul Lynde and Peter Marshall, Hollywood Squares

Hollywood Squares

One of the funniest parts of this show was the exchange between Peter Marshall and Paul Lynde. Here are a few of my favorites:

Peter: According to Ann Landers, what are the two things you should never do in bed?
Paul: Point and laugh.

Peter: In the early days of Hollywood, who was usually found atop Tony, the Wonder Horse?
Paul: My Friend Flicka.

Peter: Why do Hell's Angels wear leather?
Paul: Because chiffon wrinkles too easily.

Peter: Eddie Fisher recently states, "I'm sorry, I'm sorry for them both." Who or what was he referring to?
Paul: His fans.

Peter: In Alice in Wonderland, who kept crying, "I'm late, I'm late"?
Paul: Alice, and her mother is sick about it.

The Joke's On Me...!

Joan Rivers

Joan Rivers Jokes

When you first get married, they open the car door for you. Yesterday he opened the car door for me. We were on the freeway at the time.

When I was little, I had to beg a boy to play doctor with me. He finally agreed, and sent me a bill.

I have flabby thighs, but fortunately my stomach covers them.

They show my picture to men on death row to get their minds off women.

My best birth control now is just to leave the lights on.

A man can sleep around, no questions asked. But if a woman makes nineteen or twenty mistakes, she's a tramp.

My breasts are so low now I can have a mammogram and a pedicure at the same time.

Johnny Carson is getting so much sex he needs WD-40 on his zipper.

The Joke's On Me...!

My body is dropping so fast my gynecologist wears a hard hat.

I now consider it a good day when I don't step on my boobs.

You make the beds, you do the dishes, and six months later you have to start all over again.

My husband killed himself, and it was my fault. We were making love and I took the bag off my head.

I had a friend going through menopause come to lunch today. Her hot flash was so bad it steam-cleaned my carpet.

The Joke's On Me...!

Foster Brooks

The Joke's On Me...!

Carl Reiner

The Joke's On Me...!

You're Too Old To Trick Or Treat When...

As you're leaving your house you realize that you're walking out with a shoe on your right foot and a sneaker on your left foot.

People say, "Great mask" but you're not wearing a mask.

A candy bar dropped into your bag makes you lose your balance and fall over.

When your neighbor's door opens and you yell, "Trick or..." and then can't remember the rest.

You keep knocking on your own front door.

You're the only Power Ranger in the neighborhood with a walker.

You have to go home often to pee.

The Joke's On Me...!

Yogi Berra

Yogi Berra
(known as Yogi-isms)

You better cut the pizza in four pieces because I'm not hungry enough to eat six.

The future ain't what it used to be.

Nobody goes to that restaurant anymore. It's too crowded.

Stay alert. You can observe a lot just by watching.

Always go to other people's funerals; otherwise, they won't come to yours.

It's like déjà vu all over again.

If you come to a fork in the road, take it.

I'd give up my right arm to be ambidextrous.

The Joke's On Me...!

Rodney Dangerfield

The Joke's On Me...!

Rodney Dangerfield Jokes

When I was a kid I got no respect. I had no friends. I remember the seesaw. I had to keep running from one end to the other.

When my parents got divorced, there was a custody fight over me. No one showed up.

What a childhood I had. I was breast fed by my father.

When I was born I got no respect. After the doctor smacked me, the nurses got in a few.

I come from a stupid family. During the Civil War my great uncle fought for the west.

What a childhood I had. My parents sent me to a child psychiatrist. That kid didn't help me at all.

I was so ugly as a kid, I had to trick-or-treat over the phone.

I never got any respect from my old man. I said to him, "Nobody likes me." He said, "Don't feel that way. Everybody hasn't met you yet."

The Joke's On Me...!

Every time I leave the house, my wife tells me to call her in case something goes right.

My kid drives me nuts. For three years now, he goes to a private school. He won't tell me where it is.

What a kid I got. I told him about the birds and the bees, and he told me about the butcher and my wife.

I don't get no respect. My bank told me they'll give me a free gift if I close my account.

My wife is such a bad cook, if we leave dental floss in the kitchen, the roaches hang themselves.

During sex my wife always wants to talk to me. Just the other night, she called me from a hotel.

My wife kisses the dog on the lips, but won't even drink from my glass.

I'm telling ya, I get no respect. When I was in Switzerland, I got an obscene yodel.

I have no self confidence. When girls tell me yes, I tell them to think it over.

If it weren't for being frisked at the airport, I'd have no sex life.

The Joke's On Me...!

A girl phoned me the other day and said, "Come on over. Nobody's home." I went over. Nobody was home.

I get no respect. I was drowning, I was drowning. I kept yelling, "Help! Help!" The lifeguard came over. He said, "All right, buddy, keep it down, keep it down."

One time a guy pulled a knife on me. I could tell it wasn't a professional job. It had butter on it.

My wife's father just died. She had his body frozen. Every time I take a snack, he falls out of the refrigerator.

The Joke's On Me...!

Jack E. Leonard

Jack E. Leonard Jokes

(To Perry Como) "You have a very nice voice. Too bad it's in Bing Crosby's throat."

(To a heckler) "If there's ever a price on your head, take it."

The great Indian Chief, Falling Rocks, decided that his tribe would have to move to get food for the coming winter. He told them that he would leave and search the mountains and valleys for a place that the tribe would move to. He mounted his horse, loaded with provisions, and told his tribal leaders he would return before the full moon. Many moons passed, and the tribal leaders became worried that something had happened to Falling Rocks. So they sent scouts out to search the mountains and valleys for their chief, but to no avail. To this day the members of the tribe are still looking for him. In fact, you may still see signs that say, "What out for Falling Rocks."

(To audience) "Ladies and gentlemen, if I've said anything to offend anybody here tonight, I'd like to repeat everything I've said.

The Joke's On Me...!

More Cute Quotes

I don't mind men who kiss and tell. I need all the publicity I can get.
— Ruth Buzzi

Golf is a game in which you will yell "fore," shoot six, and write down five.
— Paul Harvey

A synonym is a word you use when you can't spell the first word you thought of.
— Burt Bacharach

If I had to live my life over, I'd make the same mistakes, only sooner.
— Tallulah Bankhead

You know your marriage is in trouble when your wife starts wearing her wedding ring on her middle finger.
— Dennis Miller

Where there's a will, there's a relative.
— Rocky Graziano

The rampant use of Viagra in nursing homes! It's like putting a flag pole on a condemned building.
— Joy Bahar

The Joke's On Me...!

A lot of people ask me how short I am. Since my last divorce, I think I'm about $100,000 short.
— Mickey Rooney

A careful driver is one who honks his horn when he goes through a red light.
— Henry Morgan

You're only young once, but you can be immature forever.
— Elizabeth McGovern

When I went to school I was so smart my teacher was in my class for five years.
— Gracie Allen

The embarrassing thing is that the salad dressing is out-grossing my films.
— Paul Newman

I'm paranoid. On my stationary bike I have a rear view mirror.
— Richard Lewis

Instead of getting married again, I'm going to find a woman I don't like and just give her a house.
— Rod Stewart

The Joke's On Me...!

Limericks

There once was an old man of Essex
Whose knowledge grew lesser and lesser.
It at last grew so small
He knew nothing at all
And now he's a college professor.

Bob went to the circus one day,
Resolved to get in without pay.
He crawled under the tent.
No one knows where he went,
For the elephants thought he was hay.

There was an old man from Nantucket,
Who kept all his cash in a bucket.
His daughter named Nan
Ran away with a man
And as for the bucket, Nantucket.

Bill Bounce, being fat for a jockey,
Tried steaming to make him less stocky.
This heated him so
That he had to eat snow
And change his profession to hockey.

The Joke's On Me...!

There was a young lady called Etta
Who fancied herself in a sweater.
Three reasons she had:
Keeping warm was not bad,
But the other two reasons were better.

There once was a fellow named Clyde,
Who went to a funeral and cried.
When asked who was dead,
He stammered and said,
"I don't know. I just came for the ride."

There once was a man name of Crocket,
Who stuck his foot in a socket.
Then along came a witch,
Who turned on the switch,
And Crocket went up like a rocket.

There was a young man with a hernia
Who said to his surgeon, "Gol-dernya.
When carving my middle,
Be sure you don't fiddle,
With matters that do not concernya."

The Joke's On Me...!

Don Rickles

Don Rickles Jokes

When you enter a room and Frank Sinatra is there, you have to kiss his ring. I don't mind, but he has it in his back pocket.

(To a heckler) If you had lived, sir, you'd have been a very sick man.

Bob Hope is so popular when he was in Vietnam they were shooting at him from both sides.

(To Burt Reynolds) Burt, in my book, you have the sexual attractiveness of a dentist's drill.

My wife takes her bra off, her head hits the sink.

(To James Arness) Arness, you've got me worried. The last time you kissed your horse, it looked like you meant it.

Italians are fantastic people, really. They can work you over in an alley while singing an opera.

The Joke's On Me...!

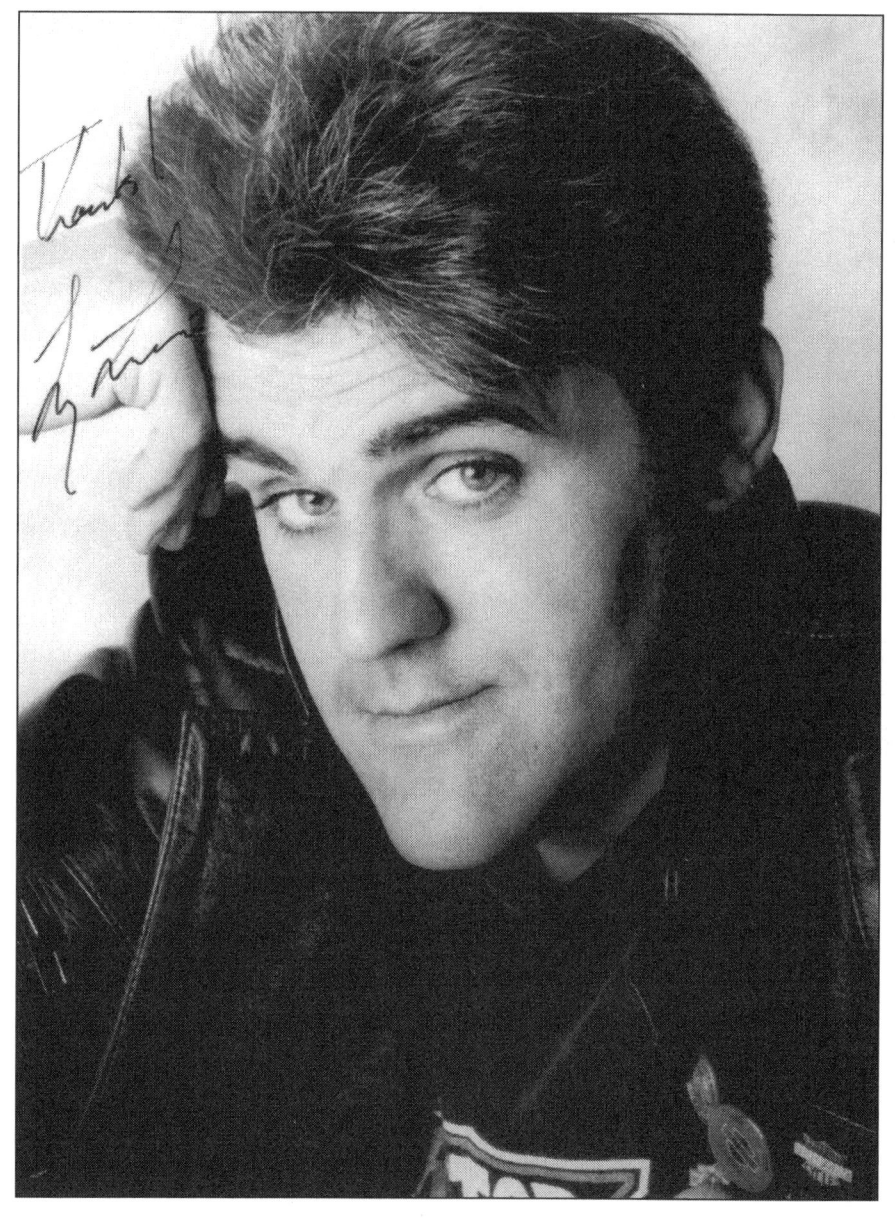

Jay Leno

Jay Leno Jokes

The Supreme Court has ruled that they cannot have a nativity scene in Washington, D.C. This wasn't for any religious reason. They couldn't find three wise men and a virgin.

Do you know how Columbus discovered America? He was drawn by the lights from the Indian casinos.

How come you never see a headline like, "Psychic Wins Lottery"?

A high school in Connecticut has a power-nap club. We called that algebra class.

Crime in New York is getting worse. I was there the other week. The Statue of Liberty had both hands up.

A man saw a problem with some railroad tracks. He took off his red shirt and waved them to stop a train from derailing. Unfortunately, he was then gored by a charging bull.

The Joke's On Me...!

Church Bulletins

Monday evening a bean supper will be held in our hall. Music follows.

Today's sermon: "Jesus Walks on Water."
Tonight's sermon: "Searching For Jesus"

At tonight's evening service, the sermon topic will be "What is hell?" Come early and listen to our choir practice.

Ladies, remember the rummage sale. It's a chance to get rid of those things not worth keeping around the house. Don't forget to bring your husbands.

While our Pastor is on vacation, massages can be given to the Church Secretary.

The ladies' Bible study will be held Thursday morning at 10. Lunch will be served in the Fellowship Hall after the ladies are done with the B.S.

Worship Reminder: The congregation is asked to remain seated until the end of the recession.

We thank our missionaries to Canada who spoke very briefly last week, much to the delight of the audience.

The Joke's On Me...!

Worry can kill you. Let the church help.

Mrs. Foster remains in the hospital and needs blood donors for more transfusions. She is also having trouble sleeping and requests CDs of the pastor's sermons.

Pot-luck supper at 5 p.m. Prayer and medication follow.

Next Tuesday there will be try outs for the choir. They need all the help they can get.

Fasting group meets for breakfast Saturday at the Pancake House.

Attend our prayer dinner next Wednesday. You will hear an excellent speaker and have a heavy meal.

Minister's new campaign slogan: "I upped my pledge. Up yours."

The Joke's On Me...!

Jewish Jokes

Yeshiva University in New York had a rowing team. They were terrible. They never won a game. And Harvard University never lost a game. They beat everybody. So the coach of Yeshivah University called a meeting of his team. He said, "Listen, I want a volunteer to go up to Cambridge and see what Harvard does. Spy on them, and come back and tell us why we lose and they always win." So one guy volunteers, and he spies on them for a week. He comes back and he says, "Coach, I found out why we lose and they win. They've got eight guys rowing and one guy yelling."

Conversation on an El Al Airplane:
    Flight attendant: "Would you like dinner?"
    Passenger: "What are my choices?"
    Flight attendant: "Yes or no."

A Jewish woman goes to her Rabbi and says, "Irving and David are both in love with me. Who will be the lucky one?" The Rabbi answers, "Irving will marry you. David will be the lucky one."

This synagogue was having a problem. There were mice running all over, and the people didn't know what to do. The Rabbi announced, "I'll take care of the problem. I know just what to do." The next day all the mice were gone. The people were amazed. They asked, "Rabbi, what did you do?" The Rabbi said, "It was simple. I bar mitzvahed them. As everyone knows, once they're bar mitzvahed, the never come back."

A Rabbi invited a blind Priest to his house for a Passover Sedar. The Rabbi placed a piece of matzah in front of the Priest. The Priest started to feel the matzah and said, "Who wrote this crap?"

Why don't Jewish mothers drink? It interferes with their suffering.

The Harvard School of Medicine did a study of why Jewish women like Chinese food so much. The study revealed that this is due to the fact that Wonton spelled backwards is "Not Now!"

The Joke's On Me...!

Mel Simons and David Brenner

David Brenner Jokes

I lived next to nine brothers. They were three months apart.

I have a brother who is twenty years older than me. Till I was eleven, I thought he was my father.

I come from a tough neighborhood in Philadelphia. I went into a bar once and said, "What do you have on ice?" The bartender replied, "You wouldn't know him."

One day, on the subway, I was sitting on a newspaper. A man came over and asked if I was reading it. What was I going to say? I'm nearsighted? Two weeks later it happens again. A man asked if I was reading the paper. I just said, "Yes," got up, turned the page, and sat down again.

You know you're getting old when you start to dress in more than six colors.

The Joke's On Me...!

Silly Signs

Sign in a drugstore: "Flu shots given while you wait"

Sign in a men's room: "Toilet out of order. Please use floor below."

Sign on the highway: "Eat here, get gas"

Sign in a bank: "Remodel your bathroom with a friendly loan. Pay as you go."

Sign on an auto repair shop: "May we have the next dents?"

Sign in a laundromat: "Automatic washing machines. Please remove all your clothes when the water goes out."

Sign in a corset store: "Gather unto you that which is yours."

Irish Jokes

A South Boston Irish bar caught on fire. The firemen rushed in, and there was a little old Irishman sitting at the bar. They carried him out, and the chief came over and said to him, "Could you tell us, sir, how the fire started?" The old Irishman said, "I don't know. It was burning when I went in there."

What's the difference between an Irish wedding and an Irish wake? One less drunk.

The phone rings at St. Mary's Church. Father Murphy picks up the phone and says, "Hello." The voice at the other end says, "Hello. Is this Father Murphy?" Father Murphy says, "Yes, it is." The voice on the other end says, "This is the Internal Revenue Service calling. Do you know a Kevin Riley, who's a member of your church?" Father Murphy says, "Yes." The IRS agent says, "Did he donate five thousand dollars to your church?" Father Murphy answered, "He will."

The Joke's On Me...!

Mel Simons and Milton Berle

Milton Berle Jokes

Your marriage is in trouble if your wife says, "You're only interested in one thing," and you can't remember what it is.

I've been married for thirty happy years, and thirty out of fifty ain't bad.

Henny Youngman is known as "The King of One Liners." That's because he can't remember two.

Youngman is the only comic that can tell four jokes in a minute, because he's never interrupted by laughs.

(To Frank Sinatra) What a crowd. I would say mob, but you know how sensitive Frank is. This aging Jerry Vale is very charitable. He built the Eisenhower Hospital in Palm Springs and put all his friends in it.

What can you say about Don Rickles that hasn't been said about hemorrhoids?

The Joke's On Me...!

Bette Midler

Bette Midler Jokes

I married a German. Every night I dress up as Poland and he invades me.

I have my standards. They may be low, but I have them.

I made a pact with myself a long time ago. Never watch anything stupider than you. It's helped me a lot.

I bear no grudges. I have a mind that retains nothing.

Elections are like dating. You pick someone who seems great, only to find out they're a jerk a few months later.

If you want something done, you'd better do it yourself – or ask another woman to do it.

After thirty, a body has a mind of its own.

Total contentment is only for cows.

We're all divine, but I was the only one who had the nerve to call myself that.

The Joke's On Me...!

Yo' Mama Jokes

Yo' Mama is so ugly... when she looks in the mirror, the reflection ducks.

Yo' Mama is so fat... when she goes to the zoo, the elephants throw her peanuts.

Yo' Mama is so dumb... she sent me a fax with a stamp on it.

Yo' Mama is so old... she has a picture of Moses in her yearbook.

Yo' Mama is so short... you can see her feet on her driver's license.

Yo' Mama is so ugly... when she was born, the doctor slapped himself.

Yo' Mama is so fat... her blood type is Ragu.

Yo' Mama is so dumb... she has to call the operator to get the number for 911.

Yo' Mama is so old... she walked into an antique store and they kept her.

Yo' Mama is so skinny... her pajamas have only one stripe.

The Joke's On Me...!

Yo' Mama is so ugly... she went to the beauty shop, and it took three hours for an estimate.

Yo' Mama is so fat... you have to take a train and two buses, just to get on her good side.

Yo' Mama is so dumb... she got locked in a grocery store and starved to death.

Yo' Mama's teeth are so yellow... when she smiles, cars slow down.

Yo' Mama is so old... when she was in school, they didn't have history.

Yo' Mama is so ugly... American Express left home without her.

Yo' Mama is so fat... she needs a watch on both arms, because she covers two time zones.

The Joke's On Me...!

Mel Simons and Norm Crosby

Norm Crosby Jokes

My school was so tough, the school newspaper had an obituary section.

Teenagers don't know what love is. They have mixed up ideas. They go for a drive and the boy runs out of gas, and they smooch a little and the girl says she loves him. That isn't love. Love is when you are married 25 years, smooching in your living room, and he runs out of gas, and she says she still loves him. That's love.

When you go into court you are putting your fate into the hands of twelve people who weren't smart enough to get out of jury duty.

Benjamin Franklin ran into the rain with a kite to give us electricity. And the kite kept slamming into the ground and pounding into the sidewalk. His wife was watching through the window and yelled, "Benjamin, you need more tail." And Benjamin yelled back, "Make up your mind. Last night you told me to go fly a kite."

The Joke's On Me...!

Buddy Hackett

Buddy Hackett Jokes

Anytime a person goes into a delicatessen and orders a pastrami sandwich on white bread, with mayonnaise, somewhere in the world a Jew dies.

I went to the doctor. I said, "Doc, my foot. I can't walk." He said, "You'll be walking before the day is over." He took my car.

As a child, my family's menu consisted of two choices: take it or leave it.

My wife said to me, "I want to be cremated." I said, "How about Tuesday?"

Did you hear what happened to Joan Rivers last night? A peeping Tom threw up on her window.

I've had a good day on the golf course when I don't fall out of the cart.

Don Rickles is the only man I know who has a film of the attack on Pearl Harbor with a laugh track.

Alan King is my fifth closest friend. He used to be seventh, but two guys went to the chair.

The Joke's On Me...!

Italian Jokes

Q: You know how American ships' names begin with "USS," which stands for "United States Service?" Then there are British ships, which names begin with "HMS" for "Her Majesty's Service." So why do Italian ships' names start with "AMB?"
A: "Att-sa My Boat"

Q: Why are Polish jokes so short?
A: It's so the Italians can understand them.

Q: What's an innuendo?
A: An Italian suppository.

Q: Why are most Italian men named Tony?
A: When they got on the boat to America they were stamped "To NY" (Tony) on their foreheads.

Q: What's a sure-fire way to know you are Italian?
A: You are 5'4", can bench 350 pounds, and you still cry when your mother scolds you.

Q: A way to know you're an Italian in the 21st Century:
A: You just tried to enter your password on the microwave.

Songs That Will Never Be Hits

"My Eyes Adored You. Tho I Never laid a Hand On You My Toes Explored You"

"You Had What It Takes, But Someone Took It"

"Is It True What They Say About Dixie? Yes, It Is. I Was Out With Her Last Night"

"You're The Reason Our Kids Are So Ugly"

"She Was From Over The Border, But Once In A While She Came Across"

"You Must Have Been A Beautiful Baby, But Baby, What Went Wrong?"

"When We Are Dancing and You're Dangerously Near Me, I Ask You Please, 'Take Off Your Skis.'"

"How Can I Miss You If You Won't Go Away?"

"Of All The Girls I've Loved Before, You're Probably Wondering What You're Scratching For"

The Joke's On Me...!

Jackie Mason

Jackie Mason Jokes

My grandfather always said, "Don't watch your money, watch your health." So one day while I was watching my health, someone stole my money. It was my grandfather.

I have enough money to last me the rest of my life, unless I want to buy something.

You can't please everybody. Like I have a girlfriend. My girlfriend to me is the most wonderful, most remarkable person in the world. That's to me. But, to my wife . . . .

My father was a very successful businessman, but he was ruined in the stock market crash. A big stockbroker jumped out of the window and fell on his pushcart.

I was so self-conscious that, when I was at a football game and the players went into a huddle, I thought they were talking about me.

A person who speaks English in New York sounds like a foreigner.

All doctors are crooks. Why do you think when a doctor writes out a prescription, only he and the druggist can read it? Because they all say the same thing: "I got my money. You get yours."

The Joke's On Me...!

Eighty percent of married men cheat in America. The rest cheat in Europe.

I have a friend who is half Italian and half Jewish. If he can't buy it wholesale, he steals it.

I have another friend who is half German and half Polish. He hates Jews, but can't remember why.

Every Jewish mother wants her son to be a doctor. If he's half retarded, a lawyer. If he has no brain, an accountant.

Did you know in my religion the sin of eating bread on Passover is comparable to the sin of adultery? I told this to a friend, and he says he tried them both and can't see the comparison.

The Joke's On Me...!

Jackie Mason

The Joke's On Me...!

Moms Mabley

The Joke's On Me...!

Moms Mabley Jokes

The only thing that an old man can do for me is tell me where to find a young one.

Anytime you see me with my arms around an old man, I'm holding him for the police.

It's no disgrace to be old. But damn if it isn't inconvenient.

My husband was so ugly he used to stand outside the doctor's office and make people sick.

(On turning down an invitation to appear for four minutes on *The Ed Sullivan Show*) Honey, it takes Moms four minutes just to get on the stage.

Pollution is so bad in New York that I saw the Statue of Liberty holdin' her nose.

The Joke's On Me...!

You Know You're Getting Old When...

You stoop to tie your shoelaces, and wonder what else you could do while you're down there.

You pay a hooker for sex and get a refund.

When you were born, the Dead Sea was just getting sick.

You get divorced and your wife gets custody of the cave.

A fortune teller offers to read your face.

You get into your car and the steering wheel is higher than you are.

Bingo has become a spectator sport.

You need to do warm-up stretches before trimming your toenails.

When the candles on your birthday cake cost more than the cake.

You spend three hours in a revolving door.

The Joke's On Me...!

The narrow waist and the broad mind begin to change places.

You know all the answers but nobody asks you the questions.

When you sink your teeth into a steak, and they stay there.

You hear "snap, crackle and pop" at the breakfast table and you're eating Cream of Wheat.

You look forward to calls from telemarketers.

Your forehead is so wrinkled you can screw on your hat.

People call you at 7 p.m. and ask, "Did I wake you?"

Your birth certificate was on a scroll.

The Joke's On Me...!

Mel Simons and Robert Klein

The Joke's On Me...!

Mel Simons and Bill Dana

87

The Joke's On Me...!

Sid Caesar and Imogene Coca

The Joke's On Me...!

Jokes

A fellow with a swollen wrist was advised by his doctor to go home and keep his wrist in a pail of extremely hot water for twelve hours. He obeyed the advice, but instead of his wrist getting better, his whole body began to swell. His maid spoke up and said, "Cold water is better than hot." He put his wrist in cold water, and all his swelling, including the wrist, stopped. Now he was angry, so he called up his doctor and shouted, "What kind of doctor are you? You told me to put my wrist in hot water, and my whole body swelled. My maid told me to put it in cold water, and I got better right away." The doctor replied, "I can't understand it. My maid said hot water."

A newly-married couple is driving in Miami Beach in a brand new car. As they're driving he puts his hand on her knee. She says, "We're married now. You can go a little farther." So he went to Ft. Lauderdale.

We asked a zoologist how porcupines have sex. He answered, "Carefully. Very carefully."

Did you hear about the three men who hijacked a truck full of Viagra? The police are looking for a gang of hardened criminals.

The Joke's On Me...!

Joe E. Lewis

Joe E. Lewis Jokes

Show me a man with both feet on the ground and I'll show you a man who can't get his pants on.

Whenever someone asks me if I want water with my scotch, I say, "I'm thirsty, not dirty."

A man is never drunk if he can lie on the floor without holding on.

I don't drink any more than the man next to me, and the man next to me is Dean Martin.

I play in the low 80s. If it's any hotter than that, I won't play.

I went on a diet, swore off drinking and heavy eating, and in fourteen days, I lost two weeks.

I told my doctor I get very tired when I go on a diet, so he gave me pep pills. Know what happened? I ate faster.

Las Vegas is the only town in the country where you can have a good time without enjoying yourself.

The Joke's On Me...!

Dick Gregory

The Joke's On Me...!

Dick Gregory Jokes

Good evening, ladies and gentlemen. I understand there are a good many southerners in the room tonight. I know the South very well. I spent twenty years there one night.

Last time I was down South, I walked into this restaurant and this white waitress came up to me and said, "We don't serve colored people here." I said, "That's all right. I don't eat colored people. Bring me a whole fried chicken."

I once sat at a lunch counter down South for nine months. They finally integrated, and didn't have what I wanted.

Where else in the world but America could I have lived in the worst neighborhoods, attended the worst schools, rode in the back of the bus, and get paid $5,000 a week just for talking about it?

I never believed in Santa Claus because I knew no white man would be coming into my neighborhood after dark.

The Joke's On Me...!

Mel Simons and Pat Cooper

94

The Joke's On Me...!

Rich Little as Jack Benny

The Joke's On Me...!

Shelly Berman and Mel Simons

Dumb Blonde Jokes

A blonde calls Delta Airlines. She says, "Can you tell me how long it takes to fly from Boston to Las Vegas?" The agent says, "Just a minute." "Thank you," the blonde says and hangs up.

How can you tell when a fax has been sent from a blonde? There is a stamp on it.

What did the blonde do when she heard that 90% of accidents occur around the home? She moved.

What are the worst six years in a blonde's life? Third grade.

Two blondes are attempting to unlock their car with a coat hanger. They had locked their keys inside the car. The first blonde said, "I don't think this is going to work." The second blonde said, "It better work. It's starting to rain and the top is down."

And then there was the blonde who was driving her friend to the airport. She saw a sign that said "Airport left," so she turned around and went back home.

The Joke's On Me...!

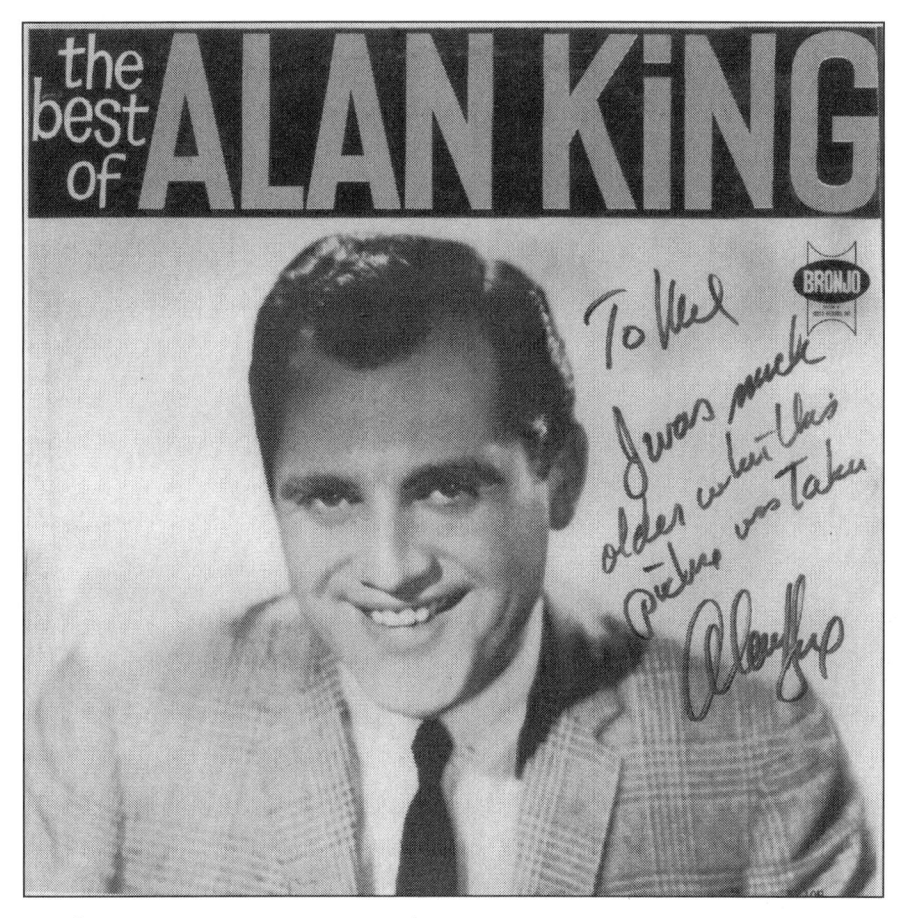

Alan King

Alan King Jokes

A middle-aged woman suffered a heart attack and was taken to the hospital. While on the operating table, she asked God if this was the end of her life. God said no, and explained that she had another thirty to forty years to live. Upon her recovery, she decided to have a face lift, liposuction, breast enlargement, and a tummy tuck. After her last operation, she walked out of the hospital. She was run over and killed by a truck. She arrived before God and said, "I thought you said I had another thirty to forty years." God replied, "I didn't recognize you."

An old man went into a confession booth and told the priest, "Father, I'm eighty years old, married, have four kids and eleven grandchildren, and last night I had an affair, and I made love to two eighteen-year-old girls. Both of them twice. The priest said, "Well, my son, when was the last time you came to confession?" The old man said, "Never, father. I'm Jewish." The priest asked, "So then why are you telling me?" He answered, "I'm telling everybody."

The Joke's On Me...!

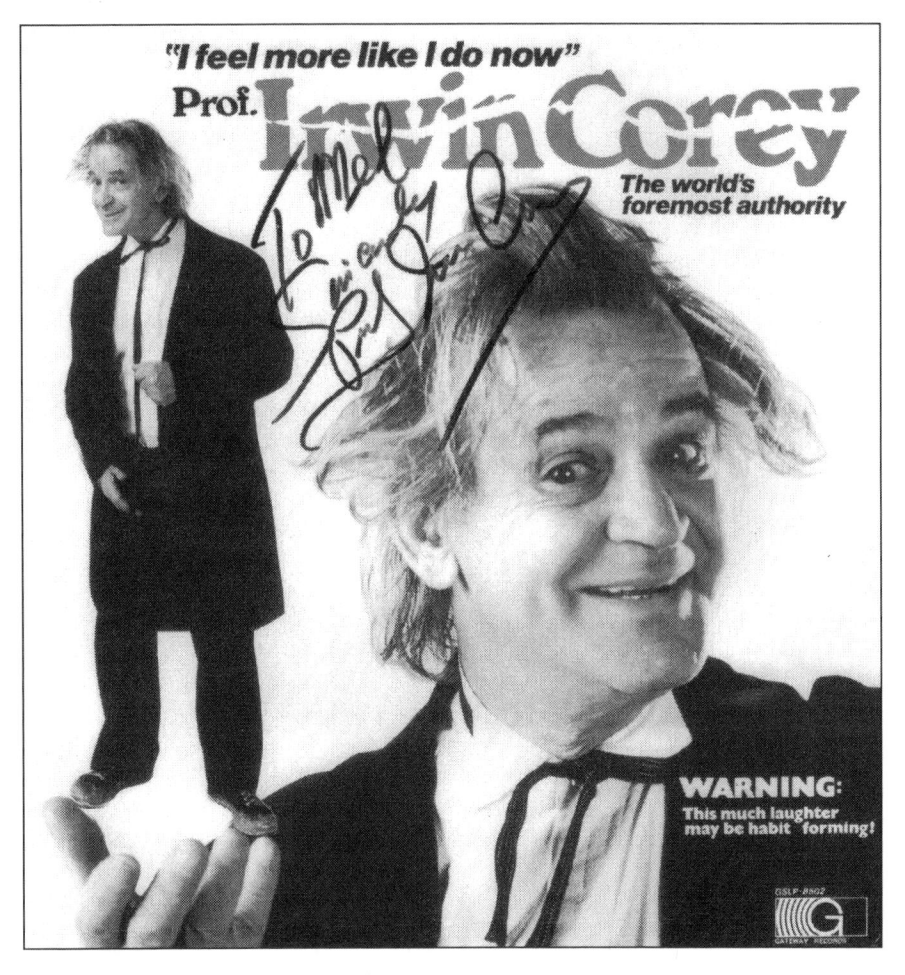

Professor Irwin Corey

Professor Irwin Corey Jokes

Sometimes I forget what I'm talking about in the middle of a word.

Ten years ago, we had Johnny Cash. We had Bob Hope and Steve Jobs. Today, ten years later, there's no cash. There's no hope. There's no jobs.

I feel more like I do now than when I first got here.

If we don't change direction soon, we'll end up where we're going.

Santa Claus? You have to look very carefully at a man like this. He comes but once a year? Down the chimney? And in my sock?

What you have to do to prevent conflict with Cuba is to shove Florida up the Mississippi, where she'll be 500 miles away.

The Joke's On Me...!

Steven Wright

Steven Wright Jokes

My girlfriend just got out of the hospital. She had to have her stomach pumped because I gave her what I thought was cotton candy, but it turned out to be insulation on a stick.

Last week the candle factory burned down. Everyone just stood around and sang "Happy Birthday."

I like to leave messages before the beep.

The guy who lives across the street from me has a circular driveway, and he can't get out.

I went to a Halloween party dressed as the Equator. People who walked toward me got warmer.

I like to fill my tub up with water, then turn the shower on and act like I'm in a submarine that's been hit.

He asked me if I knew what time it was. I said, "Yes, but not right now."

I walked up to a tourist information booth and asked them to tell me about a couple of people who were here last year.

The Joke's On Me...!

I bought some batteries, but they weren't included, so I had to buy them again.

When I woke up this morning, my girlfriend asked me, "Did you sleep good?" I said, "No. I made a few mistakes."

I'm living on a one-way dead-end street. I don't know how I got there.

I got a new shadow. I had to get rid of the other one. It wasn't doing what I was doing.

Ever notice how it's a penny for your thoughts, yet you put in your two cents? Someone is making a penny on the deal.

I talk to myself a lot and it bothers other people because I like to use a megaphone.

In my house, there's this light switch that doesn't do anything. Every so often I would flick it on and off, just to check. Yesterday, I got a call from a woman in Germany. She said, "Cut it out."

I couldn't repair your brakes, so I made your horn louder.

The Joke's On Me...!

Jokes

There was a mix-up at a swank Fifth Avenue florist shop. Wrong cards were attached to two imposing floral wreaths. The one that went to a druggist moving to a new building read, "Deepest Sympathy." The one intended for the funeral of a leading banker read, "Good luck in your new location."

A lady was taking a shower when the doorbell rang. She rushed to the door dripping wet and asked, "Who is it?" The answer came, "Blind man." She figured as long as the man was blind, there was no need to put on a robe. She opened the door and the man said, "Where do you want the blinds put, lady?"

Old man Cooperman lay on his deathbed for months and finally passed away. Two weeks later, the relatives gathered like vultures to hear the reading of the will. The lawyer tore open an envelope, drew out a piece of paper and read, "Being of sound mind, I spent every dime before I died."

The Joke's On Me...!

Phyllis Diller

Phyllis Diller Jokes

My cooking is so bad my kids thought Thanksgiving was to commemorate Pearl Harbor.

You know you're getting old when they have discontinued your blood type.

The reason women don't play football is because eleven of them would never wear the same outfit in public.

The only man who thinks I'm a ten is my shoe salesman.

I have so many liver spots I ought to come with a side of onions.

I asked the waiter, "What is this blended coffee?" The waiter said, "Yesterday's and today's."

This woman is so cross-eyed she can go to a tennis match and never move her head.

Burt Reynolds once asked me out. I was in his room at the time.

I admit I have a tremendous sex drive. My boyfriend lives forty miles away.

The Joke's On Me...!

I have a driving tip for you: Never hit the lead car in a funeral. I have never seen that many people in that bad a mood.

Last night a peeping Tom begged me to pull my window shade down.

I'm having a very bad week. My condo just went apartment.

The reason I take birth control pills is because I don't want any more grandchildren.

Fang and I are always fighting. When we get up in the morning, we don't kiss. We touch gloves.

The Joke's On Me...!

Morey Amsterdam

The Joke's On Me...!

Doctor Jokes

A man goes to the doctor and says, "Every morning I wake up and look at my face in the mirror. It makes me want to throw up. What's wrong with me?" The doctor says, "I'm not sure, but your eyesight is perfect."

A doctor says to his wife, "You're a terrible cook, you buy too many clothes, and you're a lousy lover." A week later he comes home and finds her in bed with another man. He yells, "Hey, what's going on here?" She replies, "I'm just getting a second opinion."

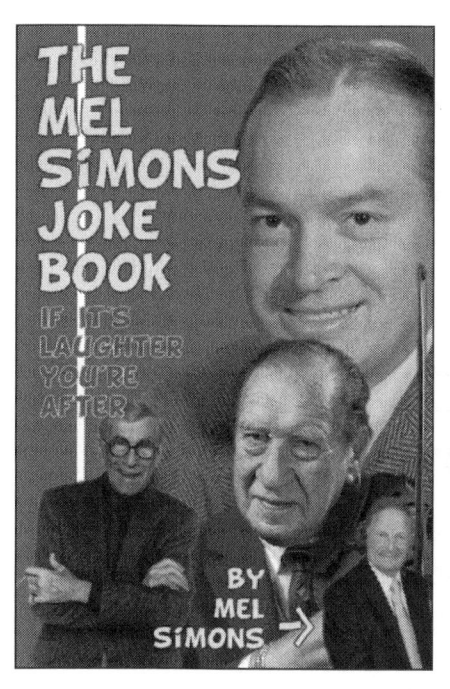

More you might like by Mel Simons!

Available at bearmanormedia.com or at MelSimons.net

All just $14.95

E-books also available!

EVEN MORE BY MEL

The Old-Time Radio Trivia Book by Mel Simons

The Old-Time Television Trivia Book by Mel Simons

Old-Time Radio Memories by Mel Simons

The Show-Biz Trivia Book by Mel Simons

Old-Time Television Memories by Mel Simons

The Movie Trivia Book by Mel Simons

Available at bearmanormedia.com or at MelSimons.net

All just $14.95

E-books also available!

SIMONS

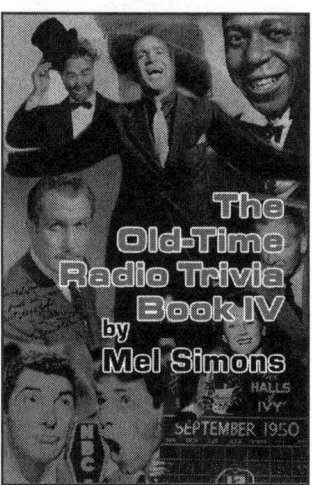

- Voices from the Philco by Mel Simons
- The Good Music Trivia Book by Mel Simons
- The Old-Time Radio Trivia Book II by Mel Simons
- The Old-Time Radio Trivia Book III by Mel Simons
- The Old-Time Radio Trivia Book IV by Mel Simons
- The Old-Time Radio Trivia Book V by Mel Simons

Made in the USA
Columbia, SC
16 March 2018